COOLNESS GRAPHED

BY RC JONES

KNOCK KNOCK®
VENICE, CALIFORNIA

Published by Knock Knock
Distributed by Who's There Inc.
Venice, CA 90291
knockknockstuff.com
Knock Knock is a trademark of Who's There Inc.

© 2013 RC Jones
All rights reserved
Made in China

Conceived and illustrated by RC Jones
coolnessgraphed.tumblr.com

No part of this product may be used or reproduced in any manner whatsoever without
prior written permission from the publisher, except in the case of brief quotations
embodied in critical articles and reviews. For information, address Knock Knock.

This book is a work of humor meant solely for entertainment purposes. In no event
will Knock Knock be liable to any reader for any harm, injury, or damages, including
direct, indirect, incidental, special, consequential, or punitive arising out of or in
connection with the use of the information contained in this book. So there.

Every reasonable attempt has been made to identify owners of copyright. Errors or
omissions will be corrected in subsequent editions.

Where specific company, product, and brand names are cited, copyright and trade-
marks associated with these names are property of their respective owners.

ISBN: 978-160106527-8
UPC: 825703-50017-2

10 9 8 7 6 5 4 3 2 1

The world changes fast, and even the coolest people can find themselves wondering if something is cool or not.

Coolness Graphed is here to help with bar charts that graph the coolness of a topic. For example, yelling "fire!" isn't cool in a theater, but it's very cool when riding on the back of a dragon.

The first graph was born out of boredom, creative frustration, and a conversation about how a whoopee cushion is cool, a whoopee couch is very cool, and Whoopi Goldberg isn't that cool at all. My need for a creative outlet and an outpouring of fan support have kept the graphs coming—with inspiration found in pop culture, news, history, art, conversations, and boring meetings.

Seven months after sketching the first graph, I created the Coolness Graphed blog on Tumblr. Since then, the graphs have been covered by Forbes, MSN, GraphJam, and plenty of sites that focus on esteemed topics like "Funniest cat falls."

Use this book if you want to know what's cool, or already know but need a printed source to back you up. Use it to make a point, or to make others laugh. Use it to balance out a coffee table, either by placing it under a wobbly leg or on top next to books that take themselves too seriously.

It's also the perfect gift for the person who has everything except an answer to what to release at a wedding. And if you know any kids that love bar charts, this is the ultimate bedtime storybook.

In short, share and enjoy these graphs however you see fit.

Stay cool.

RC Jones

CAT PEOPLE

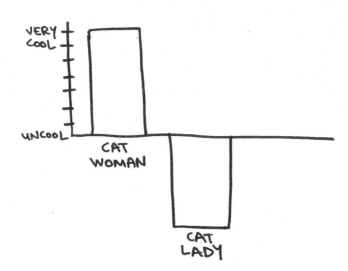

THINGS TO RELEASE AT A WEDDING CEREMONY

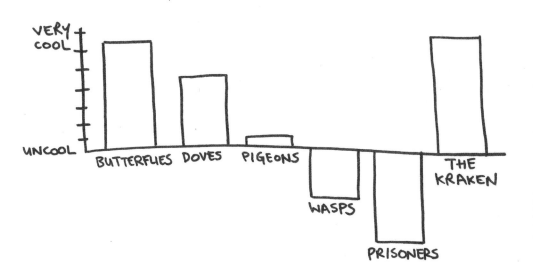

GOVERNMENT

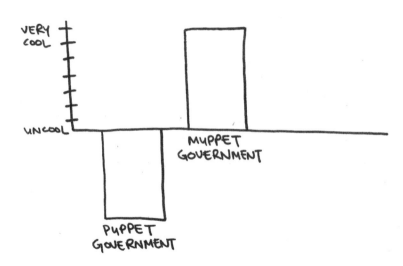

BEING SPINELESS

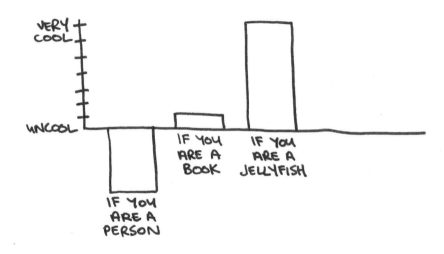

WAKING UP TO A BEAR CLAW
IN YOUR FACE

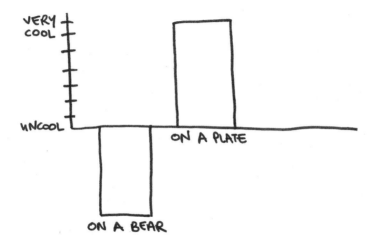

PLACES TO BE DISCOVERED

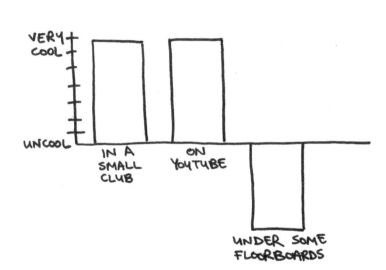

WINNING THE LOTTERY

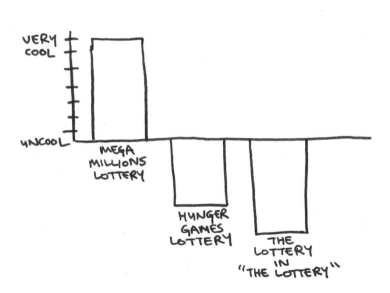

LYING ON THE BEACH

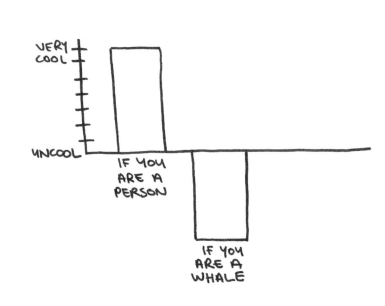

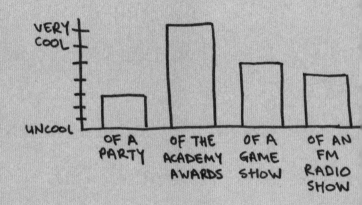

BEING THE HOST

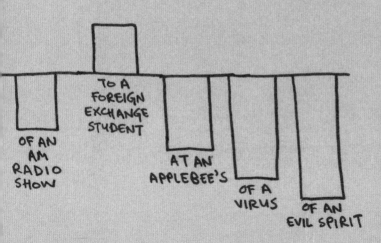

EATING TO SOLVE PROBLEMS

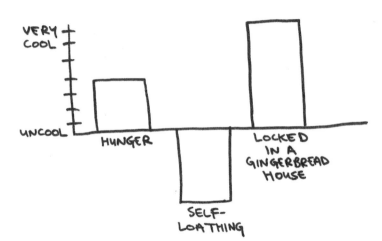

COOLNESS OF NOT CARING

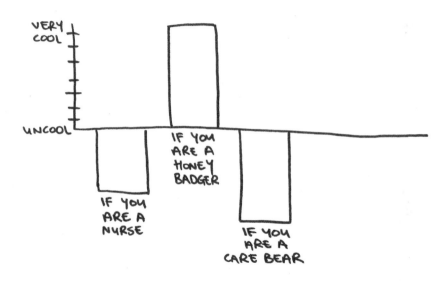

DOING THE MOONWALK

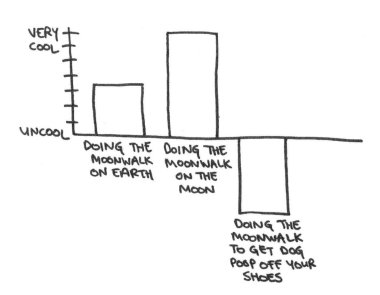

INSTANCES IN WHICH TO CALL GHOSTBUSTERS

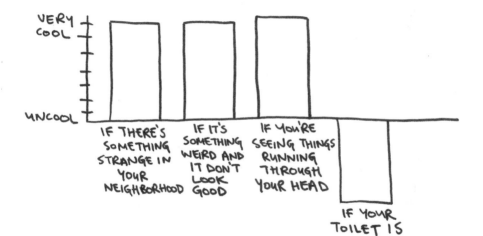

PIÑATA CONTENTS

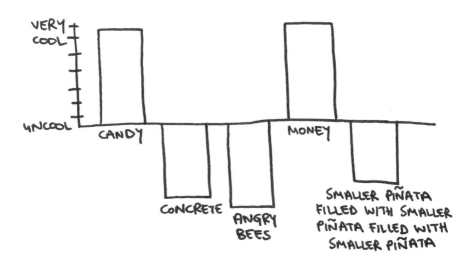

VERY COOL

COOL

UNCOOL

CANDY

CONCRETE

ANGRY BEES

MONEY

SMALLER PIÑATA FILLED WITH SMALLER PIÑATA FILLED WITH SMALLER PIÑATA

HATE CORRESPONDENCE

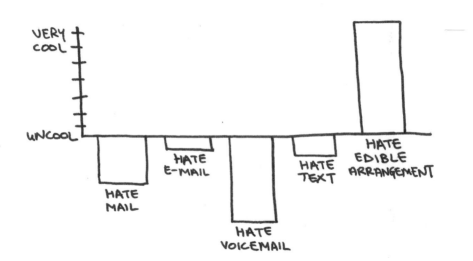

HEARING "HEADS! TAILS!"

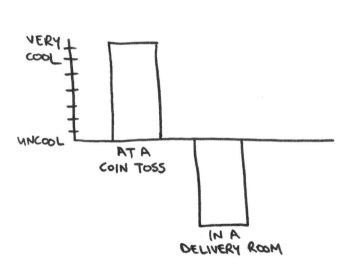

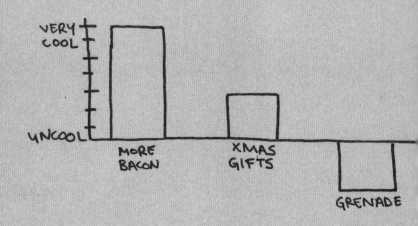

OBJECTS WRAPPED IN BACON

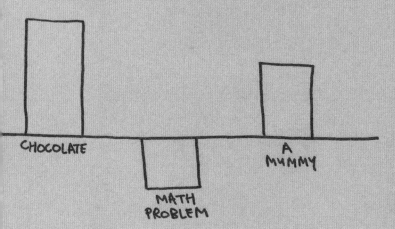

CHOCOLATE

MATH
PROBLEM

A
MUMMY

YELLING "FIRE!"

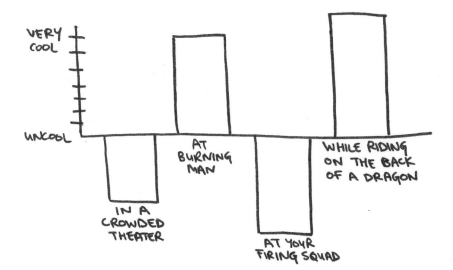

UNTITLED

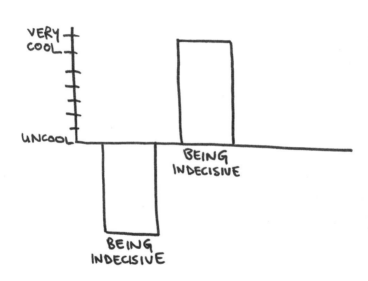

HAVING YOUR ARM IN AN
UPRIGHT CAST

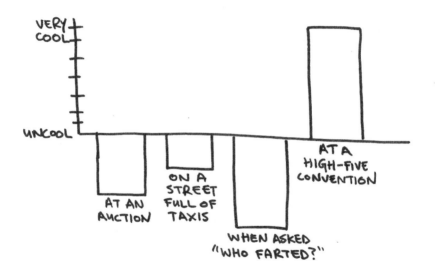

FINDING A PICKLE

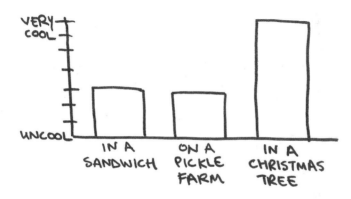

ACTIVITIES TO DO ON A ROOF

TASTES LIKE CHICKEN

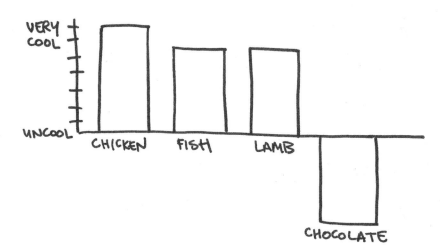

THINGS TO PUSH DOWN THE STAIRS

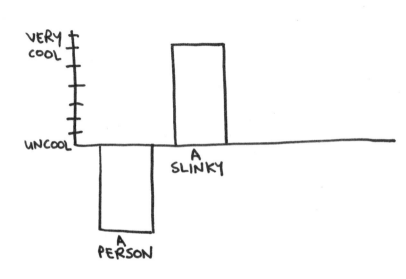

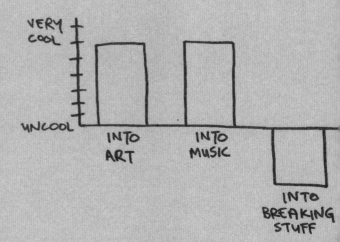

CHANNELING ANGER

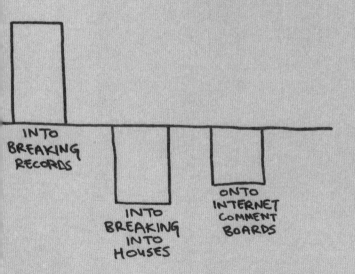

INTO
BREAKING
RECORDS

INTO
BREAKING
INTO
HOUSES

ONTO
INTERNET
COMMENT
BOARDS

WINE

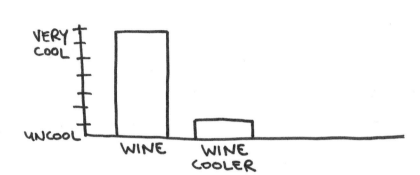

THROW PILLOWS

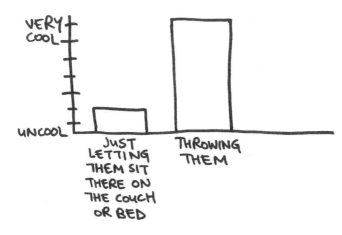

HORNS

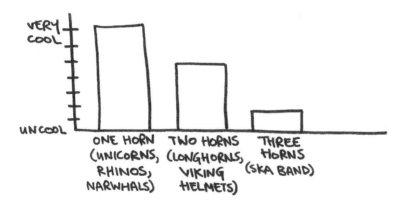

PEOPLE WHO PUT BABY
IN A CORNER

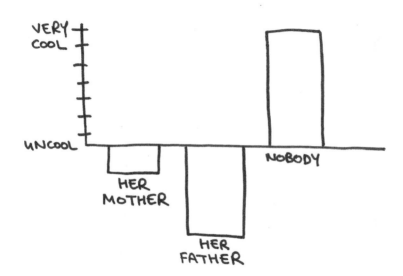

MUFFIN TOPS

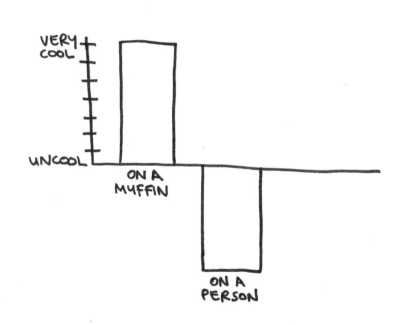

BEING BLINDFOLDED AND
TAKEN SOMEWHERE

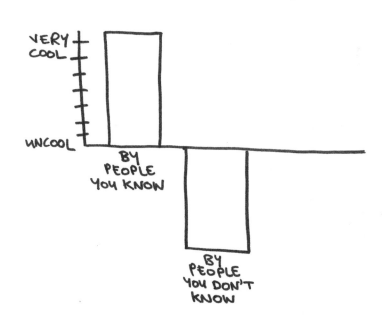

CREATING A BAR GRAPH

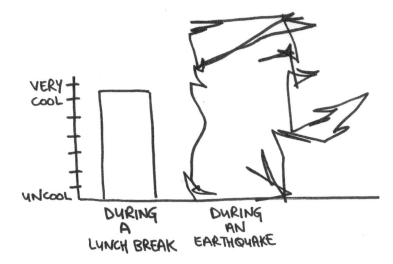

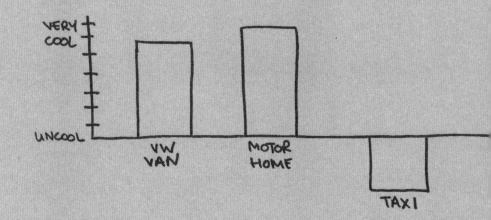

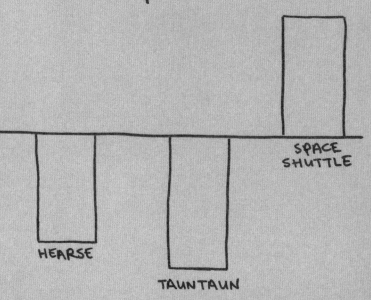

THINGS TO RUN OUT OF

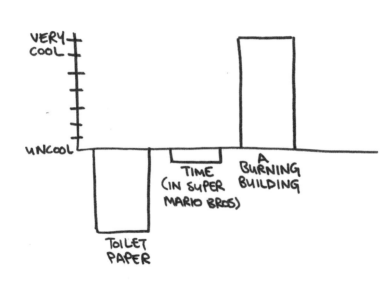

LIFTS

THROWING A DRUMSTICK
INTO A CROWD

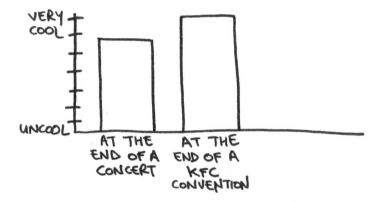

HAVING POOP IN YOUR PANTS

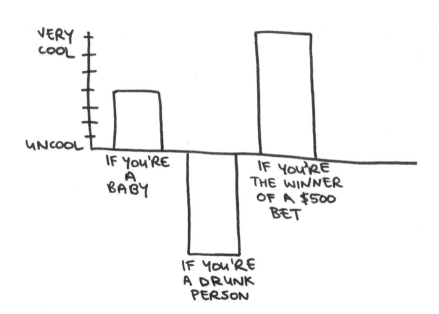

TMNT

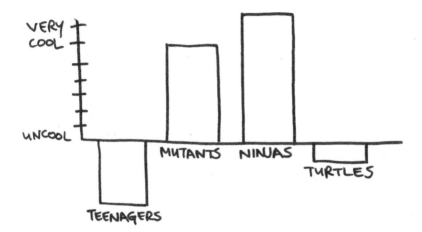

JUDGING A BOOK BY ITS COVER

VERY
COOL
UNCOOL
IF YOU'RE A JUDGE IN A BOOK COVER ART CONTEST
ANY OTHER TIME

THIRD WHEEL

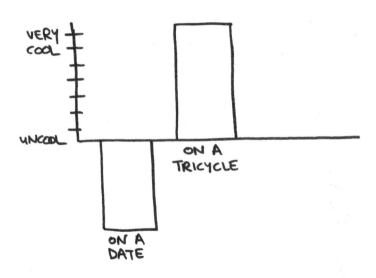

THINGS TO NICKNAME

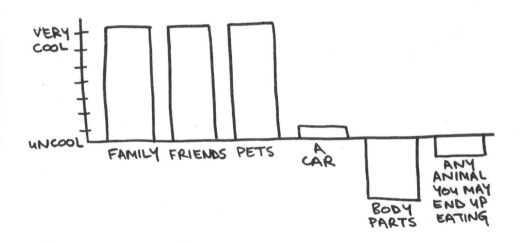

A PONYTAIL

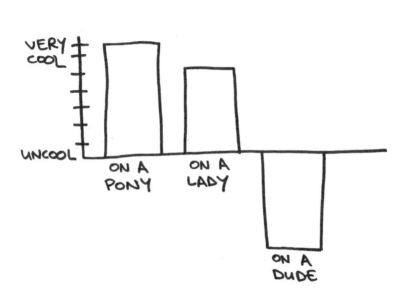

PEOPLE

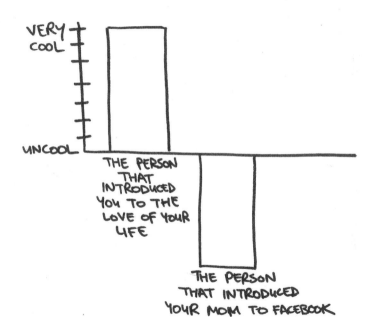

ZOMBIES

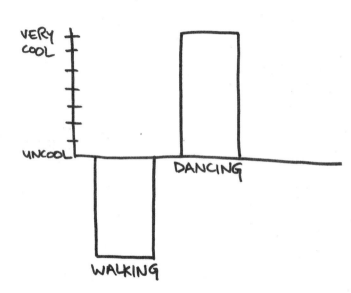

SUITS

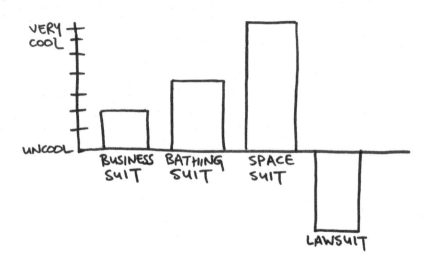

DOTTING AN I WITH A HEART

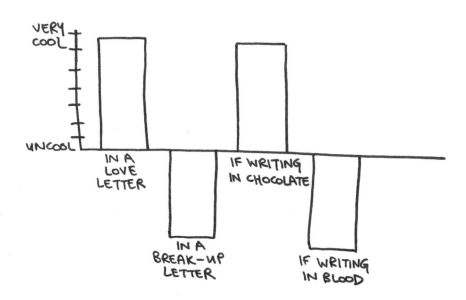

THINGS WITH WHOOP

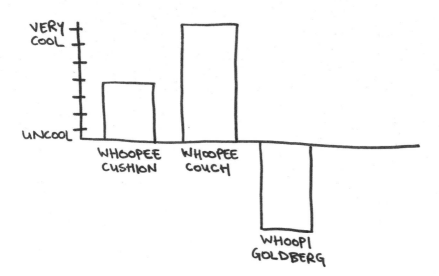

COWBELL

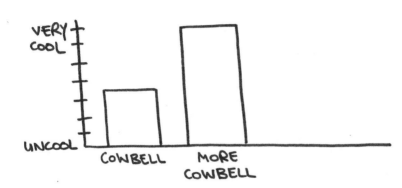

COFFEE-TABLE BOOKS

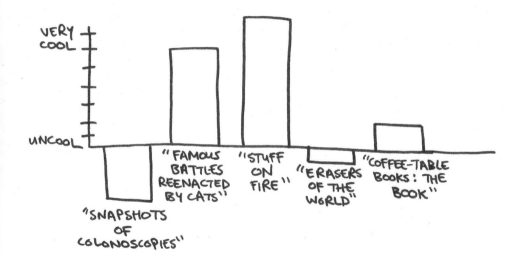

VERY COOL

UNCOOL

"SNAPSHOTS OF COLONOSCOPIES"

"FAMOUS BATTLES REENACTED BY CATS"

"STUFF ON FIRE"

"ERASERS OF THE WORLD"

"COFFEE-TABLE BOOKS: THE BOOK"

GRAPHS

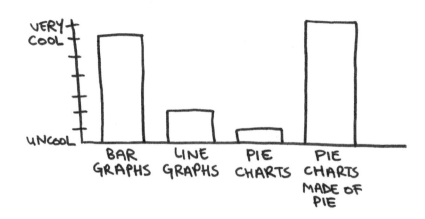

VERY COOL

UNCOOL

BAR GRAPHS | LINE GRAPHS | PIE CHARTS | PIE CHARTS MADE OF PIE

ACKNOWLEDGMENTS

Thanks to Dave Theibert, JZ, Lauren Schroer, Nick Seaman, and Jason Oberholtzer. Thanks to my wife (for embracing my warped mind), my mom and dad (for raising said mind), and my siblings (for tolerating said mind). Thanks to Jeni, Tara, Joshua Wentz, Maves, Heddy, and my agent Susan Schulman. And lastly, thanks to my kindred spirits, the very cool folks at Knock Knock.